Celebrating your year

1951

a very special year for

A message from the author:

Welcome to the year 1951.

I trust you will enjoy this fascinating romp down memory lane.

And when you have reached the end of the book, please join me in the battle against AI generated copy-cat books and fake reviews.

Details are near the back of the book.

Best regards,
Bernard Bradforsand-Tyler.

Contents

1951 American Family Life	8
Austerity in the United Kingdom	13
Our Love Affair with Cars	16
The Golden Age of Television	20
Most Popular TV Shows of 1951	21
Everybody Loves Lucy	23
Korean War Intensifies	26
The Cold War–Nuclear Arms Race	30
Nuclear Testing in Nevada	31
The Red Scare and the Rosenbergs	33
Churchill Returns to Power	35
Apartheid Laws in South Africa	36
Chinese Rule Over Tibet	39
1951 Sci-Fi Inspired Films	41
1951 in Cinema and Film	42
Top Grossing Films of the Year	43
A Streetcar Named Desire	45
The King and I Broadway Triumph	48
Musical Memories	51
1951 Billboard Top 30 Songs	52
Fashion Trends of the 1950s	56
An Artificial Heart Machine	64
Inaugural Pan American Games	66
Other Sporting Events from 1951	67
Other News from 1951	68
Famous People Born in 1951	72
1951 in Numbers	76
Image Attributions	84

Advertisement

HOME... on a 3 minute pass

..and the things we make help them get there

Whether making home seem closer, or speeding production, or coordinating defense—what a vast network of Bell telephone equipment it takes to bring people together 145 million times a day! As manufacturing unit of the Bell System, Western Electric makes the good, dependable equipment that does the job.

Western Electric

MANUFACTURING AND SUPPLY UNIT OF THE BELL SYSTEM

Home...on a 3 minute pass...and the things we make help them get there

Whether making home seem closer, or speeding production, or coordinating defense—what a vast network of Bell telephone equipment it takes to bring people together 145 million times a day! As manufacturing unit of the Bell System, Western Electric makes the good, dependable equipment that does the job.

Western Electric
Manufacturing and Supply Unit of the Bell System

Let's flashback to 1951, a very special year.

Was this the year you were born?

Was this the year you were married?

Whatever the reason, this book is a celebration of your year,

THE YEAR 1951.

Turn the pages to discover a book packed with fun-filled fabulous facts. We look at the people, the places, the politics and the pleasures that made 1951 unique and helped shape the world we know today.

So get your time-travel suit on, and enjoy this trip down memory lane, to rediscover what life was like, back in the year 1951.

1951 American Family Life

Imagine if time-travel was a reality, and one fine morning you wake up to find yourself flashed back in time, back to the year 1951.

What would life be like for a typical family, in a typical town, somewhere in America?

A family cooling off outside their home in the 1950s.

The post-war boom continued throughout the entire decade of the '50s, giving us booming birth numbers, booming suburbs, a booming economy, and the booming trappings of the consumerist culture we still enjoy today. With the stringent post-war years well behind us, the rising middle classes were feeling an urgent need to spend.

An unprecedented 3.83 million babies were born in 1951 (up from 2.8 million at the end of the war six years earlier).[1]

To cater to the increase in demand, new houses were built in record numbers, most of them in the new suburban developments springing up on the outskirts of towns. Home sales were boosted by returned soldiers who had access to low interest loans through the G.I. Bill (1944-1956). A house in the suburbs quickly became the American dream for white middle-class families.

Artist's impression of a family outing in 1950s America.

The family was everything. Fathers commuted to earn a salary. Wives were encouraged to quit their jobs and stay at home. Children walked to school and played outdoors in their well manicured gardens.

Families dined together, watched television together, and enjoyed leisure time and outings together.

The average family income was $3,700 a year.[2] Unemployment was 3.1% and falling, with GDP growth at 8%.[3]

Average costs in 1951 [4]	
New house	$9,000
New car	$1,500
Vacuum cleaner	$15
Pop-up toaster	$21
A gallon of gasoline	$0.27

[1] U.S. Census Bureau *Estimates of the Population of the United States*: 1950-1954, page 2.
[2] census.gov/library/publications/1953/demo/p60-012.html.
[3] thebalance.com/unemployment-rate-by-year-3305506.
[4] thepeoplehistory.com and mclib.info/reference/local-history-genealogy/historic-prices/.

Advertisement

THE PASADENA—For a Narrow Lot—

Price Given On Enclosed Price List
WE PAY THE FREIGHT

Here is a home of ultra-modern design that can be placed either way on your lot. Frontage required can be as narrow as forty feet, or when placed the long way on your site, can still occupy a fifty foot lot. Take especial note of the large picture window, in size, from floor to ceiling. You may have this window either as shown in the photo above or we will transpose it to the rear of the living room and place the mullion window, now in the back, at the end of that room. Plan No. 2 provides three bedrooms although it is the smaller of the two plans. Specifications will be furnished on request. Write us.

PLAN No. 1

PLAN No. 2

The Pasadena–For a Narrow Lot–Price Given on Enclosed Price List

Here is a home of ultra-modern design that can be placed either way on your lot. Frontage required can be as narrow as forty feet, or when placed the long way on our site, can still occupy a fifty foot lot. Take especial note of the large picture window, in size, from floor to ceiling. You may have this window either as shown in the photo above or we will transpose it to the rear of the living room and place the mullion window, now in the back, at the end of that room. Plan No. 2 provides three bedrooms although it is the smaller of the two plans. Specifications will be furnished on request. Write us.

Appearing in a 1951 Aladdin Homes mail-order catalog, Aladdin's Readi-Cut Homes came as a build-it-yourself kit of pre-cut lumber, plaster, shingles, plaint, etc. Every piece was numbered and crated, and arrived with full instructions. From 1906 to 1982, Aladdin sold over 75,000 kit homes in the USA and Canada.

Joining the television in our families' list of must-haves were: fully-automatic washing machines, front-loading dryers, defrost refrigerators, vacuum cleaners, air-conditioning and heating units, milkshake makers, and a multitude of other kitchen gadgets and home appliances. In addition we needed a family car or two, bicycles, motorcycles, hiking and camping equipment, picnic gear, and much, much more.

An energetic and persuasive advertising industry, through TV, radio and print, ensured we always knew what our next purchase should be.

A Bendix automatic dryer, 1951.

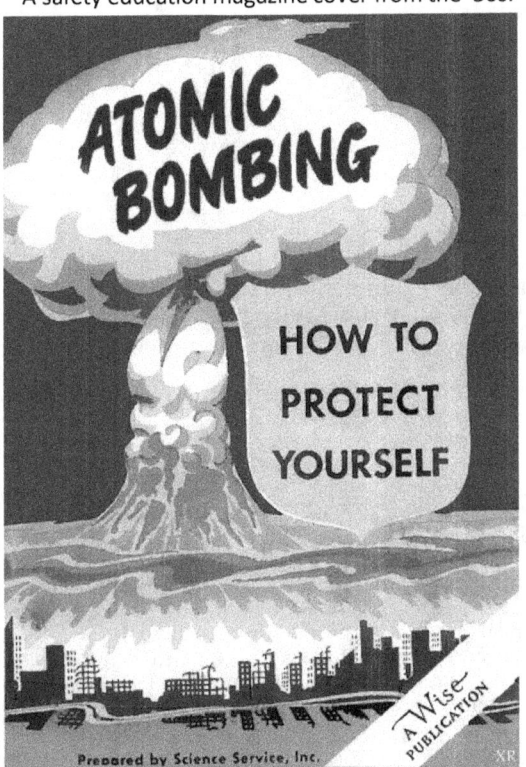

A safety education magazine cover from the '50s.

But beneath the appearance of abundance and domestic bliss, Americans were deeply concerned. The Soviets had detonated an atomic bomb in 1949, setting in motion a nuclear race between the two superpowers—the Cold War.

By 1951 both powers were striving to build an even more powerful weapon—the hydrogen bomb.

We would endure another 40 years of tension between the two super-powers before the Cold War finally ended with the dissolution of the Soviet Union in 1991.

Advertisement

No other washer gives you such a perfect combination of washing advantages!

This is IT! The washer designed with YOU in mind... the 1951 Thor Spinner Washer with Hydro-Swirl Action! Four wonderful features are combined in this one wonderful washer! *Only Thor gives you all 4!*

Hydro-Swirl washing action! The Thor has it... the super-efficient Hydro-Swirl principle of washing. Thor lets the water do the work. It swishes and swirls clothes gently but thoroughly... actually washes clothes cleaner, faster, yet is safer for fabrics. And proved best by test in laboratory and home!

Saves 27 gallons of hot water! The 1951 Thor beats the 8 other leading automatic or semi-automatic washers in economy! Saves up to 27 gallons of hot water every washday for a family of 4! Proved by test! And Thor saves soap, saves fuel costs, too.

Controllable washing time! No fixed mechanical cycles that must be gone through. With the 1951 Thor, *you* decide how much water—*you* decided how long to wash each load. Then flick the switch. Thor washes and rinses, then spins your clothes damp dry—in one single tub! Your hands never touch hot, soapy water!

Thor-way overflow rinse! Look! Dirt and suds float up and off the top, *not down through the clothes,* as in ordinary washers. And the 1951 Thor has finger-tip control... lets you rinse (as well as wash) for as long or short a period as you like.

No Plumbing Installation Necessary! No Bolting Down! No Annoying Vibration!

Austerity in the United Kingdom

Now just imagine you flashed back to a town in 1951 United Kingdom or Western Europe.

Unlike boom-time America, a very different, more restrained lifestyle would await you.

London, like many other major European cities, bore the brunt of destruction from WWII bombings. Reconstruction was painfully slow, hampered by a general shortage of money, manpower and materials.

In cities there was a desperate shortage of housing to accommodate the growing population. Nearly half of those in cities lived in private, rented, often substandard apartments. While in the country, homes often lacked water, sanitation, electricity and phones.

A London street scene in 1950.

Stifling and miserable austerity measures, in place since the start of the war, were slowly being lifted. By 1951, most items were available for purchase without coupons, however rationing of meat and sugar would continue for a few more years.

The post-war baby boom, along with a shortage of funds and building materials for new schools, often resulted in crowded classes of up to 50 students in urban areas. Only 30% of 15-year-olds, 14% of 16-year-olds and 7% of 17-year-olds remained in full time education.[1]

British children at school in the early '50s.

Snap elections held in October 1951, just 20 months after the February 1950 elections, saw the ruling Labour Party lose to the Conservatives. Winston Churchill, UK Prime Minister from 1940-1945, would be reinstalled for an additional four years from 1951-1955.

Within months, Churchill traveled to the USA for talks with President Truman, with the aim of renewing UK's "special relationship" with America, and to discuss joint strategies for communism containment.

[1] researchbriefings.files.parliament.uk/documents/SN04252/SN04252.pdf.

Advertisement

INTERNATIONAL HARVESTER
REFRIGERATORS

Ahead in Quality

Ahead in Convenience

Ahead in Features

Ahead in Design

Color-Keyed TO YOUR KITCHEN!

Now... Rainbow Hues to Accent Refrigerator Door Handles

Now you can have color in your refrigerator to match your kitchen! For the door handle, choose from ten beautiful hues to complete your color scheme. And you can change color in the handle any time. It's an IH exclusive!

MODEL HA-92
Capacity 9.2 cubic feet

Handy Butter Keeper built in spot, holds *full pound of butter*! Keeps at creaming consistency. (Model HA-92)

Built-In Bottle Opener built into cabinet frame. Magnetized, on Model HA-92 to keep caps from falling.

they're *femineered!*

FEMINEERING AT ITS FINEST—Pantry-Dor shelves give convenient, front-row storage... full-width Freezers hold up to 50 lbs.... Coldstream Crispers keep vegetables and fruit fresher, longer... Stainless Steel Shelves... Egg-O-Mat, Diffuse-O-Lite, Shadowline styling and other great IH exclusives!

FAMOUS IH QUALITY—from *top to bottom, inside and outside*—for excellent service year in, year out!

SEVEN MODELS! SEVEN SIZES! SEVEN PRICES! —to suit every family, every home, every budget. See all seven new beauties at your IH Refrigerator dealer's today.

INTERNATIONAL HARVESTER COMPANY

International Harvester Refrigerators
Ahead in Quality   Ahead in Convenience   Ahead in Features   Ahead in Design
Color-Keyed to your Kitchen!

Now... Rainbow Hues to Accent Refrigerator Door Handles, *they're femineered!*

Femineering at its finest–Pantry-Door shelves give convenient, front-row storage... full-width Freezers hold up to 50lbs... Coldstream Crispers keep vegetables and fruit fresher, longer... Stainless Steel Shelves... Egg-O-Mat, Diffuse-O-Lite, Shadowline styling and other great IH exclusives!

Famous in quality–*from top to bottom, inside and outside*–for excellent service year in, year out!

Seven models! Seven sizes! Seven prices!–to suit every family, every home, every budget. See all seven new beauties at your IH Refrigerator dealer's today.

Our Love Affair with Cars

In just five years since war's end, the US car industry had shifted from fabricating utilitarian war tanks and trucks, to producing fashionable consumer vehicles, the kind of which we just had to have. More than 80% of cars globally were produced in the USA, a figure that has been in decline ever since, as other countries advanced their car industries.

There were now 42.5 million registered cars on US roads, up from 25.7 million at war's end.[1] Our love affair with cars was firmly entrenched.

Cars on a Philadelphia traffic circle in the early '50s.

Detroit had long been the car manufacturing hub of the country, and America led the world in car production, turning out 7.2 million vehicles in 1951 alone.[2] This equated to almost 80% of all new vehicles worldwide.

With population peaking in 1950-'51 Detroit was now the 5th largest city in the US.[3] And by the end of the decade, a whopping one in six adults nation-wide would be employed in the car industry.

[1] fhwa.dot.gov/ohim/summary95/mv200.pdf.
[2] en.wikipedia.org/wiki/American_automobile_industry_in_the_1950s.
[3] theweek.com/articles/461968/rise-fall-detroit-timeline.

Our love affair with cars grew hand-in-hand with the post-war baby boom and housing construction boom. Where would we be without our cars? How else could we get from our far-flung suburban homes to our inner city offices?

Now–get the Plus of a Packard at the price of a car!

Above–1951 Packard Patrician 400.

Left–1951 Studebaker Commander.

Studebaker again amazes America!

Rising incomes ensured the family car was increasingly affordable. An additional 2.34 million vehicles were put on the US roads as families fled the cities for the quiet life of the suburbs.

1951 Hudson Step-down.

Cars were no longer just a necessity; they had become an expression of our personality. Sturdy, sporty, or luxurious, cars now came in a wide range of styles, colors, and price points, with chrome, wings, stripes and fins for added personality.

"Nothing like it for Long Life"
Here's the one for the long run-mile after mile-year after year-it's engineered to last!
New 1951 Mercury   Nothing like it on the Road!

From the stitches in its seats to the head bolts on its power plant, Mercury is *precision-built* for the years ahead of it. For long-run investment, you're smart to put your money in this penny-pincher!

Mercury stays new longer—keeps upkeep low and trade-in value high—goes easy on gas—gives you what you want and deserve from a 1951 car.

You get a great new car that *looks* the part. There's a sweep of motion in its line and a sense of power in its look. But *Mercury's* beauty goes far deeper than that—it's built into every part of the car!

Drive a Mercury first chance you get. Test the whisper-hustle of its great 8-cylinder, V-type engine. Check the broader, softer seating—the new increased visibility—the extra roominess. Then you be the judge. You'll decide Mercury's got what you want—and you'll enjoy it for many years to come!

Advertisement

Cuts 92% of your driving motions! New Fordomatic Drive does your gear shifting for you. It's America's newest, finest, most flexible automatic transmission!

Stretch your driving dollars–with Ford's Automatic Mileage Maker! You get high-compression performances with regular gasoline! A new Waterproof Ignition System prevents engine "shorts" from moisture.

No car is better finished, better built! There's quality that lasts in the quiet elegance of Ford's new Luxury Lounge interior, in the soundness of Ford's coachwork!

Enjoy "Fashion-Car" styling–from the new recessed headlights to new Jet-Styled Windsplits. Ford's designed to stay "right" in the years ahead!

Feel the safety of an extra-heavy steel Luxury Lifeguard Body! And Ford's new Double-Seal King-Size Brakes keep out dirt and water–give smooth, safe stops in any weather!

"Test Drive" the '51 Ford... at your Ford Dealer's today. And as your drive it, remember that this car is built for the years ahead! With 43 "Look Ahead" features, it was planned and engineered to stay young in performance, to stay in style, to stay thrifty–for years to come! Relax with Ford's new Automatic Ride Control! It adjusts your ride to any road automatically! The going stays easy, level–no pitch, no jounce, no roll!

All the best for the years ahead   You can pay more but you cant buy better '51 Ford

The Golden Age of Television

The television set quickly became the centerpiece of every family home. By 1951, 10.3 million American households, equivalent to 23.5% of the population, owned a television set, (an increase from 3.88 million households, or just 9% of the population 12 months earlier).[1] And that number would rise exponentially through-out the decade as television became our preferred choice of entertainment.

Family focussed Motorola television advertisements from 1951.

For the rising middle classes, television was much more convenient than going to a downtown cinema. It provided an increasing array of programs to watch, it was available every day of the week, and it was free to watch once purchased.

[1] americancentury.omeka.wlu.edu/items/show/136.

Most Popular Television Shows of 1951

1	Arthur Godfrey's Talent Scouts	11	Mama
2	Texaco Star Theater	12	Philco TV Playhouse
3	I Love Lucy	13	Amos 'n' Andy
4	The Red Skelton Show	14	Gangbusters
5	The Colgate Comedy Hour	15	Big Town
6	Arthur Godfrey and His Friends	16	Goodyear TV Playhouse
7	Fireside Theatre	17	Pabst Blue Ribbon Bouts
8	Your Show of Shows	18	The Lone Ranger
9	The Jack Benny Show	19	Gillette Cavalcade of Sports
10	You Bet Your Life	20	All Star Revue
		=	Dragnet

* From the Nielsen Media Research 1951-'52 season of top-rated primetime TV series in the USA.

In the early '50s television continued to rely on live broadcasts of popular radio programs, as these were faster to produce, and cheaper than new made-for-TV dramas.

Comedy-Variety programs remained our most popular form of family-time TV entertainment, accounting for six of the top eight programs for the year.

Dean Martin and Jerry Lewis in *The Colgate Comedy Hour* (NBC. 1950-1955).

Also keeping us glued to our screens were highly rated drama series such as *Fireside Theater* (NBC. 1949-'58), *Philco TV Playhouse* (NBC. 1948-'55), *Goodyear TV Playhouse* (NBC. 1951-'57), and *The Lone Ranger* (ABC. 1949-'57).

Clayton Moore and Jay Silverheels in *The Lone Ranger* (ABC. 1949-1957).

Jack Webb in *Dragnet* (NBC. 1951-70, Syndication. 1989-91, ABC. 2003-04).

Lynn Loring and Mary Stuart in *Search for Tomorrow* (CBS. 1951-82, NBC. 1982-86).

The television networks were quick to turn out new programs to keep us tuning in. Here are just a few of the new programs that aired for the first time in 1951: *Dragnet, The Red Skelton Show, Search for Tomorrow (35 seasons), I Love Lucy, Hallmark Hall of Fame, What's My Line* (UK), and *Crazy People* (UK).

Red Skelton in *The Red Skelton Show* (NBC. 1951-1971).

Peter Sellers, Harry Secombe, Spike Milligan, & Michael Bentine, in *Crazy People* (later *The Goons*, BBC. 1951-60).

Everybody Loves Lucy

15th October 1951

In mid-October 1951, Lucille Ball launched onto our screens and into our hearts as New York housewife Lucy Ricardo, along-side real-life husband Desi Arnaz, in the sitcom *I Love Lucy*.

Spanning six seasons, the groundbreaking sitcom was the first scripted television program to be filmed in front of a live television audience. It would become the most watched TV show in 4 out of its 6-year run. Three film cameras allowed for multiple angle capture of every scene, a standard technique still used in sitcom production today.

The main cast in an episode from 1955.

Ball continued her comedic genius for CBS with *The Lucille Ball-Desi Arnaz Show* (1957-1960), *The Lucy Show* (1962-1968), and *Here's Lucy* (1968-1974). In 1986, ABC aired the 8 episode *Life with Lucy*.

The cast of *I Love Lucy*: William Frawley, Desi Arnaz, Vivian Vance and Lucille Ball.

A total of 180 half-hour *I Love Lucy* episodes were filmed, still watched around the world today as re-runs.

I Love Lucy holds the honor of being the first TV show to be inducted into the *Television Academy Hall of Fame* (1951).

In 2012 the show was ranked the Best TV Comedy and the Best TV Show in *Best in TV: The Greatest TV Shows of Our Time*.

Advertisement

Better looking in every way!
RCA Victor Million Proof television–proven in over a million homes

They "look like a million"–and they're Million Proof–the new RCA Victor television receivers!

Any one you choose gives you the best in picture quality, styling and performance. And no wonder! They're built from RCA Victor's experience in producing *well over a million* television receivers.

All have the new, extra-powerful RCA Victor circuits for peak performance. The fabulous RCA Victor television pick-up brings in the picture even in "fringe" areas. All have the rich, true-to-life tone of RCA Victor's famous "Golden Throat" acoustical system. All have decorator cabinets–styled to "live with" the finest of modern or traditional furnishings.

And–*only* when you buy RCA Victor television can you buy the RCA Victor Factory- Service Contract for expert installation and maintenance.

Advertisement

But for him... words would be sterile, meaningless things... words like freedom, liberty, justice, equality... words that make pacts, proclamations, constitutions, charters... hopes for a better, more peaceful future.

Back of each man with a gun there are at least 25 men in uniform. They are men who are doers in their own right... specialists in communications, transportation, engineering, food, housing, motors, maintenance, repairs, electronics and many others.

Today's Army is a multiple combination of teams... in which all individuals merge their identity for a cause. Yet, as on any team in civilian life, individuals emerge from the group to carry the team and the cause.

Your Army is constantly seeking individuals of courage and initiative. Last year more than 200,000 men volunteered for the role of HIM. If you believe you can qualify, stop in at your nearest U.S. Army and U.S. Air Force Recruiting Station and see how much your Army offers you!

Korean War Intensifies   1950-1953

American forces entered the Korean War in June 1950, to assist South Korea with expelling Communist invaders from the north. By the start of 1951, the South Korean, US and UN forces were exhausted from the relentless battles against the powerful North Korean military (KPA).

While the Allies fought for a return to the Post War status quo of two Koreas divided along the 38th Parallel, the KPA was determined to unite Korea as one country under communist rule.

With financial backing from the Soviets and China, the KPA first captured Seoul in June 1950, holding the capital for 3 months before being pushed back northwards to the border with China.

Crew of an M24 tank along the Naktong River front, 24th August 1950.

Soldiers take cover behind a tank during an attack. Hongchon area, 22nd May 1951.

Chinese forces entered the war in large numbers at the end of 1950, joining the KPA to push south and recapture Seoul. January to April 1951 saw the Chinese launch a Third, Fourth and Fifth Offensives in quick succession on the embattled southern divisions.

In contrast to the well equipped and well trained KPA, the South Korean military forces were ill prepared and outnumbered.

US supplied machinery and artillery took several months to obtain. As fresh US Army and Marine Corps units arrived, they brought with them much needed tanks, antiaircraft guns, rocket launchers, jets and bombers.

A Hawker Sea Fury FB.11 fighter from British aircraft carrier HMS Glory, 1st June 1951.

An F4U-4B Corsair of Squadron 113 (VF-113) flies over US ships at Inchon, 15th Sept 1950.

Joining the war effort were a UN combined force from twenty-one countries including the UK, Australia, Canada, France, Philippines, and Thailand.

Outnumbered on the ground, the UN forces exploited their superior air power, dominating the skies in the early months of the war.

Air combat quickly became deadlier as Chinese and Soviet jet fighters took up battle. US pilots conducted night-time bomb raids, venturing deeper and deeper into North Korea to destroy enemy targets.

A total of 635,000 tons of bombs were dropped on North Korea, turning nearly every city and village to rubble. Citizens were advised to dig tunnels to live in.

In addition, the US dropped 32,557 tons of lethal napalm.

A US Air Force Fighter Bomber releases two napalm bombs over North Korean industrial military targets, Jan 1951.

The city of Seoul was captured 4 times during the first 12 months of battle. Casualties of war saw an estimated 1.68 million South Korean lives lost.

Food shortages and lack of housing were severe.

Left: Korean girl with baby brother on her back walks by a stalled M-46 tank at Haengju, 9th June 1950.

Below left: Medical corpsmen helping wounded infantrymen, following the fight for Hill 598, 14th Oct 1952.

Below: A grief-stricken infantryman whose buddy had been killed in action, Haktong-ni area, 28th Aug 1950.

More than 3 million people lost their lives during the war, of which half were civilians from both South and North Korea. Causes of death included bombings, massacres, starvation and disease.

The war unofficially ended in July 1953 with the creation of the Demilitarized Zone separating the two Koreas. To date no peace treaty has been signed, leaving the two Koreas technically still at war.

Advertisement

Bombs Away!

That terse report from bombardier to aircraft commander on the B-50 intercom means: "Mission accomplished!" It marks the climax of a Strategic Air Command mission... pushed through by men with guts, despite enemy flack and fighters. It means another blow at the enemy's power to strike.

As the bombardier speaks, all across the formation bombs slant toward the earth, five weather-dark miles below, pulled forward by the 450-mile-an-hour speed of the giant aircraft. This is the moment of climax.

But back of that dramatic moment is a long history of planning and preparation. Top-notch design... top-flight training... and the raw courage of men who make your U.S. Air Force the best in the world.

Top Aviation Cadet training produced this B-50 team's Aircraft Commander and Pilot... taught Navigator, Bombardier and Radar Officer to work interchangeably in one another's jobs. Great Air Force schools trained the Airman crew... flight engineer, radio operator, central fire control man, gunner-electrician.

And, behind them all... the vast organization of your modern Air Force has worked toward that moment of climax. Radar, radio maintenance, weather, intelligence... all pointed for that report by the bombardier: "BOMBS AWAY!"

The Cold War–Nuclear Arms Race

Cold War tensions between the two former allies–the USSR and the USA–had been increasing since the end of the war in 1945. Starting in the USA as policies for communist containment, the distrust and misunderstanding between the two sides quickly escalated from political squabbling, to a military nuclear arms race. For more than 40 years, the Nuclear Arms Race gave the two superpowers the pretext needed to test nuclear bombs on a massive scale.

After the first atomic (fission) bombs dropped on Hiroshima and Nagasaki in 1945, the US continued testing nuclear bombs on land, sea and air.

The Soviets tested their first atomic bomb in August 1949. The Nuclear Arms Race was underway.

On 31st January 1950, President Truman gave the green light to develop a much more powerful thermonuclear hydrogen (fusion) bomb. Ivy Mike, the world's first hydrogen bomb, was detonated in 1952. The mushroom cloud from the 10.4 megaton bomb rose 41 km (25.5 mi), with a radius of 161 km (100 mi).

More than 2,000 nuclear bombs have been tested since 1945, with millions of people unwittingly exposed to radioactive fallout over the years.

Ivy Mike atmospheric nuclear test, 1st Nov 1952.

Military personnel watch a nuclear explosion in the Nevada Deseret, 1957.

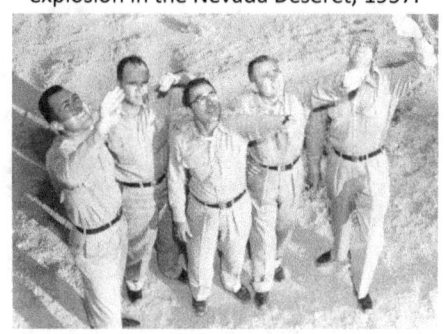

By 1950, the US had amassed a stockpile of 299 nuclear weapons. The Soviets were just ramping up, with 5 nuclear weapons at the start of the decade, increasing their stockpile to 1,605 by decade's end.

Both sides continued to increase their nuclear stockpiles. The US peaked in 1967 with a total of 31,225 weapons, against the Soviet's 8,339 weapons.[1] The USSR continued to grow their stockpile until 1988 (amassing 23,205 weapons). In 1991, the Nuclear Arms Race ended with the signing of a denuclearization treaty.

[1] tandfonline.com/doi/pdf/10.2968/066004008.

Nuclear Testing in Nevada   27th January 1951

The Nevada Proving Grounds were established for the explicit purpose of testing nuclear devices. The Grounds covered 1,360 square miles of desert and mountain terrain in Nevada, Las Vegas.

Operation Buster-Jangle was the first US nuclear field exercise conducted on land. Troops observed the blast from 6 miles away, 1st Nov 1951.

Commencing on 27th January, a series of 5 bombs were dropped from B-50D bombers and exploded in open air. Over the next 41 years, a total of 1,021 nuclear tests would be carried out here. Of these, 100 were atmospheric tests, carried out prior to 1963 when the *Limited Test Ban Treaty* brought an end to atmospheric testing.

Mushroom clouds from atmospheric tests could be seen from Las Vegas, leading to an increase in tourism. Hotels promoted mushroom cloud viewing parties, advertising the detonation times for advanced bookings.

It is estimated that millions of Americans were unwittingly exposed to the radioactive iodine fallout from the bombs.

Las Vegas tourist postcard, 1951.

Advertisement

the beauty of it...

Telechron® can't run wrong!

ELECTRIC CLOCKS AND THEY START AT $4.50*

IVY Perfect gift to grace her kitchen. Hangs on wall or sets on shelf. Takes real vines in twin vases color-styled in red, grey, yellow. $7.95*

AIRLUX Gift of elegance. For bedroom, mantel, desk. Rich hand-rubbed mahogany finish case. Bell alarm. $17.50*

Telechron electric clocks are silent. Need no winding, oiling, regulating. Choose from 29 lovely models for every room in the house. Full-year written warranty. Famous Telechron Synchro-Sealed Motor is synchronized perfectly with electric power plants so it has to run right! Telechron is a trademark of Telechron Inc., Ashland, Mass., a General Electric Affiliate.

Telechron Electric Clocks can't run wrong! And they start at $4.50

Ivy. Perfect gift to grace her kitchen. Hangs on wall or sets on shelf. Takes real vines in twin vases color-styled in red, grey, green, yellow. $7.95.

Airlux. Gift of elegance. For bedroom, mantel, desk. Rich hand-rubbed mahogany finish case. Bell alarm. $17.50.

Telechron electric clocks are silent. Need no winding, oiling, regulating. Choose from 29 lovely models for every room in the house. Full-year written warranty. Famous Telechron Synchro-Sealed Motor is synchronized perfectly with electric power plants so it has to run right!

The Red Scare and the Rosenbergs

In the early '50s, American politicians repeatedly warned the public to be fearful of the Communist influence. Communists could be lurking anywhere, living and working among us, aiding the Soviets in their quest for world domination. During 1951 this paranoia reached new heights when Julius and Ethel Rosenberg were convicted of spying for the Soviets.

Julius Rosenberg was accused of leading a network of spies, several of whom had been arrested a year earlier on suspicion of passing top-secret information to the Soviets. This information included American designs on the construction of nuclear weapons.

His wife was accused of assisting in her husband's spy network.

Julius and Ethel Rosenberg, separated by heavy wire screen in the US Court House, after being found guilty by jury, 1951.

The trial of the Rosenbergs in March 1951 lasted just three weeks. They were found guilty of espionage and condemned to die in the electric chair, making them the only two American civilians to be executed for espionage-related activity during the Cold War.

Documents released decades later proved Ethel Rosenberg's role in her husband's activities were minor and limited. Her conviction and execution were wrongful. She had been framed by her brother and sister-in-law, who were themselves spies in the same network.

Advertisement

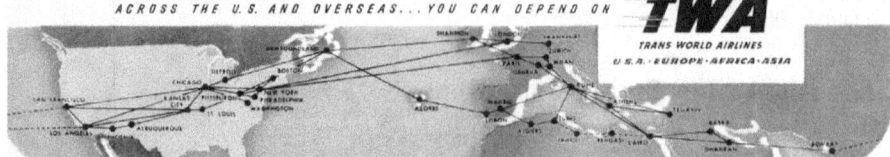

Grandma leads a fast life... and loves it!

No one has to go home to see Grandma today because now *she's* going... by Skyliner. Age simply doesn't matter. From the moment she settles in her comfortable seat until the family waves hello, Grandma is in good hands. A thoughtful TWA hostess is always nearby, anticipating every need. And best of all, TWA's direct routes across the U.S. end any worries about changing places or transferring baggage. It's easy and fun traveling TWA–for *all ages*. Grandmas love it!

Where in the world do you want to go? For flight information and reservations call TWA or your travel agent.

Across the U.S. and overseas... you can depend on TWA

Churchill Returns to Power

25th October 1951

The British general election of October 1951 saw Winston Churchill's Conservative Party return to power with a slim majority of seats, despite not winning the popular vote. It marked the start of a 13-year rule by the Conservatives. Churchill, 76 years old, would remain in power a further four years, resigning in 1955 due to health concerns.

During this period Churchill made four trips to America. Although on good terms with both President Truman and later President Eisenhower, the Americans knew the Empire was in decline, and did not wholly support Churchill's commitment to ongoing British imperialism.

Churchill was UK Prime Minister from 1940-1945 and 1951-1955. He led the Conservative Party for 15 years (having led the Liberal Party for 20 years earlier).

Churchill with Americans General (later President) Dwight D. Eisenhower and Field Marshal Bernard Law Montgomery, 19th Oct 1951.

Churchill had served as an army officer and war correspondent in British India, Anglo-Sudan and the Second Boer Wars. He was also a writer, receiving a Nobel Prize for Literature in 1953.

Churchill is remembered as a great war-time leader.

Churchill wearing Garter robes, with his son and grandson standing behind.

Apartheid Laws in South Africa

The Afrikaner National Party of South Africa came to power in 1948 with "apartheid" (apartness) as their slogan and political goal. White supremacist laws were immediately enacted to reinforce white minority rule and divide non-whites along color and tribal lines. The following years saw numerous Acts come into effect, to strengthen the apartheid rule.

The creation of the *Group Areas Act* (1950) and the *Prevention of Illegal Squatting Act* (1951) ensured 80% of the land was reserved for exclusive ownership by the ruling white minority.

These Acts allowed for forcible, often violent, removal of non-whites from white designated areas. Evictions of entire suburbs, destruction of property, fines and criminal arrests became commonplace over the following years.

Area warning signs were commonplace.

The voting rights of blacks and mixed-race were removed with the *Separate Representation of Voters Act* (1951). Interracial marriage or sex was prohibited. Access to schools and other facilities were separately designated. Even access to employment was controlled. The Native Building Workers Act (1951) allowed for Blacks to access training for certain types of semi-skilled jobs but limited the areas they were permitted to work.

Protest marches and police action in South Africa in the early '50s.

These Acts were strengthened and amended multiple times over subsequent years.

Following decades of international condemnation and sanctions, the laws were finally repealed in 1991 with the dismantling of South Africa's Apartheid system.

Advertisement

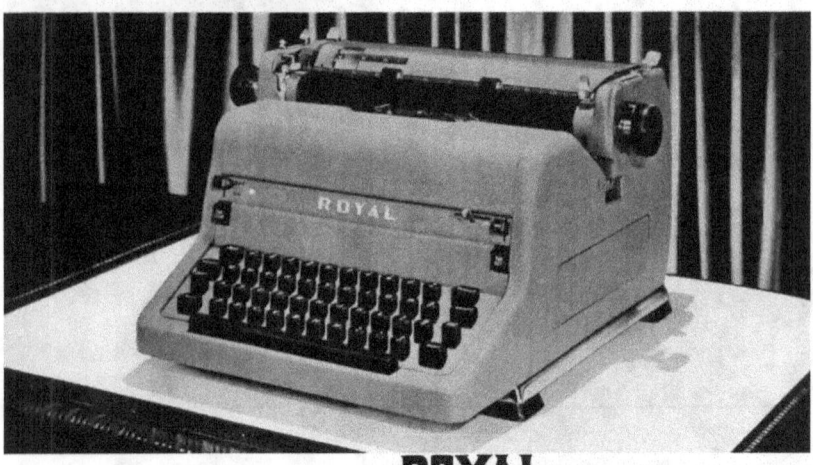

ROYAL Electric Typewriter

Smart girls want the best...

Of course, you choose clothes that bring out your best point... whether it's a dinner date or a day at the office. Why not take the same angle toward your office typewriter? Decide on the new Royal Electric. It brings out your best points as an up-and-coming secretary. It was designed with you in mind. The Royal Electric Typewriter is newly designed throughout, so that electricity does the work for you! Tension and fatigue are well-nigh banished... and you *feel* better and *look* better, when five o'clock rolls around. And what a joy to operate! The controls are in the same positions as on your favorite Royal Standard Typewriter. There's virtually no "change-over" problem. What a break to be on familiar ground.

Now, you ask, how about the work? It pours out... literally. As many as 20 carbon copies, too. Your letters sparkle with a crisp clarity that does you credit. Heavy-duty work is delivered with remarkable speed and efficiency. Exclusive "Touch Control" allows you to adjust the touch to give you the "feel" you prefer. Exclusive "Magic" Margin permits instant, automatic margin setting.

The Royal Electric is *your* typewriter... because of its many exclusive features... because it was designed with *you* in mind. So–choose the finest. Choose Royal.

Chinese Rule Over Tibet   23rd May 1951

After months of Chinese military occupation, delegates from the Buddhist mountain nation of Tibet were summoned to Beijing to negotiate a peace deal. They were then presented with a document known as the *Seventeen Point Agreement for the Peaceful Liberation of Tibet*, which was duly signed on 23rd May 1951. Under the terms of the Agreement, Tibet now officially belonged to China.

The Chinese government claimed that Tibet was always a part of China. However Tibet's government-in-exile maintains their representatives were forced to sign the Agreement, rendering it invalid.

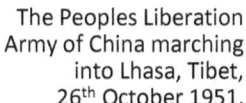
The Peoples Liberation Army of China marching into Lhasa, Tibet, 26th October 1951.

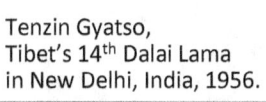
Tenzin Gyatso, Tibet's 14th Dalai Lama in New Delhi, India, 1956.

Chinese rule included socialist land reforms, torture, public humiliations, suppression of religion, and military crackdowns over any resistance.

During the decade, Tibetan resistance guerrillas, with financial support from the CIA, fought against Chinese occupation. Tibetan exiles claim that more than one million have died at the hands of the Chinese since 1951.

During 1959, fearing for his life, Tibet's spiritual leader– the Dalai Lama–fled to India.

GIVE **EVERSHARP** AND YOU GIVE THE FINEST

You write better with this new Eversharp because...

it's the world's only pen with Magic Feed! –this prevents flooding, leaking or skipping–and gives your words instant starting, smooth flow, clean ending! Because no other pen gives you all these great writing features Compare...and see for yourself!

Here is a writing instrument you have to handle before you can believe it. Designed with the world's easiest-writing features–magnificent in its jewel-like beauty–the new Eversharp gives you lifelong satisfaction...the only pen tested and approved by the U.S. Testing Company for its excellent craftsmanship and writing qualities.
• Special Breather Tube–Insures largest ink capacity ever. Yours only with Eversharp. • Hand Wrought Points–14 kt. Gold–extra-large–in your choice of styles to fit your individual writing. • Positive Flip-Fill–Fast, sure, safe. Nothing to take apart or put together. Just flip the lever–pen's brim-full.
• $8.75 Complete set–handsomely gift-packaged. Pen alone, $5.00

Give Eversharp–and you give the finest

1951 Sci-Fi Inspired Films

The Day the Earth Stood Still by 20th Century Fox.

The Man from Planet X by United Artists.

Flight to Mars by Monogram.

When Worlds Collide by Paramount.

1951 in Cinema and Film

Scene from *Quo Vadis* (MGM. 1951).

Highest Paid Stars

1. John Wayne
2. Dean Martin
=. Jerry Lewis
4. Betty Grable
5. Bud Abbott
=. Lou Costello

Having reached its peak in the mid-1940s, cinema attendance faced a steady decline throughout the 1950s. With more and more families filling their leisure time with the convenience of television, the motion-picture industry sought new ways to win over new audiences.

Younger audiences now had cash to spare. Movie themes adjusted to accommodate the new trends in popular culture, and to exploit the sex appeal of young, rising stars such as Marilyn Monroe, James Dean and Marlon Brando.

Dean Martin, Jerry Lewis and Marilyn Monroe at the 1953 Redbook Awards.

Grace Kelly in 1951.

1951 film debuts

Jeff Bridges	The Company She Keeps
Charles Bronson	You're in the Navy Now
Leslie Caron	An American in Paris
Grace Kelly	Fourteen Hours
Leonard Nimoy	Queen for a Day
William Shatner	The Butler's Night Off

* From en.wikipedia.org/wiki/1951_in_film.

Top Grossing Films of the Year

1	Quo Vadis	MGM	$11,143,000
2	Show Boat	MGM	$5,293,000
3	David and Bathsheba	20th Century Fox	$4,720,000
4	The Great Caruso	MGM	$4,309,000
5	A Streetcar Named Desire	Warner Bros.	$4,250,000
6	The African Queen	United Artists	$4,100,000
7	That's My Boy	Paramount	$3,800,000
8	An American in Paris	MGM	$3,750,000
9	A Place in the Sun	Paramount	$3,500,000
10	Father's Little Dividend	MGM	$3,122,000

* From en.wikipedia.org/wiki/1951_in_film by box office gross in the USA.

MGM's musical comedy *An American in Paris* won seven of its nine nominations.

The lavish historical epic *Quo Vadis* was the run-away box office success of the year, bringing in over $11 million in US ticket sales and nearly as much at the foreign box offices. The film was nominated for eight Academy Awards, but failed to win any.

Advertisement

Sally Forrest's silky-soft golden hair ripples with sparkling waves. See how lovely Rayve Creme Shampoo makes your hair—how easy to curl

Young Hollywood stars agree that

No other shampoo makes your hair so shining clean... so easy to curl!

Young Hollywood stars agree that

No other shampoo makes your hair so shining clean... so easy to curl.

The absolutely perfect shampoo–that's what Hollywood's young beauties have christened Rayve Creme Shampoo! They adore the sparkling new highlights... the soft, fresh beauty of Rayve-clean hair. And Rayve leaves your hair so soft and lively–just ready to fall into nice deep waves!

Now–see the new beauty Rayve gives your hair! Fresh and shining, gloriously clean, dancing with light... eager to curl! Rayve's unique balanced formula combines *deep-cleaning* lather with rich *curl-conditioning* oils... coaxes out shining new-found waves and curls you never *dreamed* you had.

The limp wave test will show you! Give yourself a Rayve Creme Shampoo at the very *end* of your permanent–when your wave's all but gone! You'll see how Rayve revives your wave–washes new sparkle into your hair. Get a tube or jar of Rayve Creme Shampoo today... and see how it makes even a tired wave just *want* to curl!

A Streetcar Named Desire

18th September 1951

Vivien Leigh as Blanche DuBois in *A Streetcar Named Desire* (Warner Bros. 1951).

Based on Tennessee Williams' 1947 Pulitzer Prize-winning play, the 1951 film version of *A Streetcar Named Desire* cast Marlon Brando, Kim Hunter, and Karl Malden in their original Broadway roles. The lead role for heroine Blanche duBois was given to Vivien Leigh, who previously played the role in London's West End.

Brando was a relatively unknown actor at the time of casting. He received his first Oscar nomination for his performance.

Cinema poster from 1951.

The controversial themes tackled in the play—suicide, homosexuality, and rape—were largely ignored or lightly passed over in the movie, in order to conform to the Motion Picture Production Code.

A Streetcar Named Desire has since been preserved by the US Library of Congress National Film Registry.

Marlon Brando from the Broadway theatre production *A Streetcar Named Desire*, 1948.

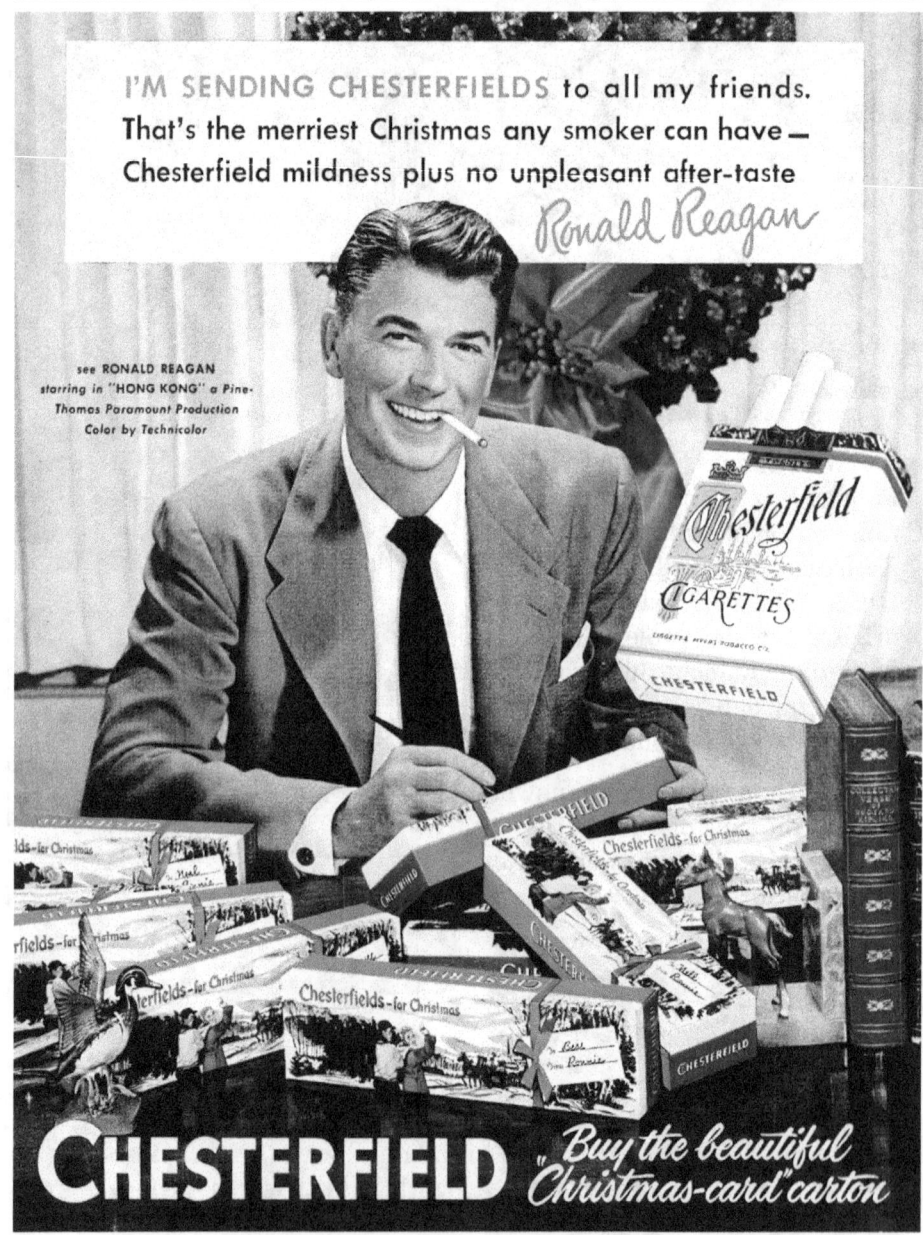

I'm sending Chesterfields to all my friends.
That's the merriest Christmas any smoker can have–
Chesterfield mildness plus no unpleasant after-taste   Ronald Reagan

See Ronald Reagan starring in "Hong Kong" a Pine-Thomas Paramount Production. Color by Technicolor.

Chesterfield   *Buy the beautiful "Christmas-card" carton*

Advertisement

Mrs. Humphrey Bogart (Laruen Bacall) says

Lauren Bacall, speaking for style-wise women everywhere, endorses The New Idea in Smoking from the feminine point of view... As for men, they go in a big way for delicious smoking pleasure in a shape, trim and handy as a cigarette... The *perfect mild* smoke.

Convenient as a cigarette...
Fits neatly between the smoker's lips, or into a holder.

Humphrey Bogart and his wife, Lauren Bacall, co-stars of Santana Pictures, are both ardent, expert sailors.

Robt. Burns Cigarillos 5¢ each
"In a class by itself"

The King and I Broadway Triumph 29th March 1951

Gertrude Lawrence and Yul Brynner pose in full costume for *The King and I* original stage production.

The King and I opened on Broadway's St. James Theatre on 29th March 1951 to triumphant reviews. It would run for 3 years, winning Tony Awards for Best Musical, Best Actress (Gertrude Lawrence) and Best Featured Actor (Yul Brynner). The crowd pleaser was later made into a film (1956), continued with a national tour, and saw numerous stage revivals.

Oscar Hammerstein (standing) with Richard Rodgers (at the piano).

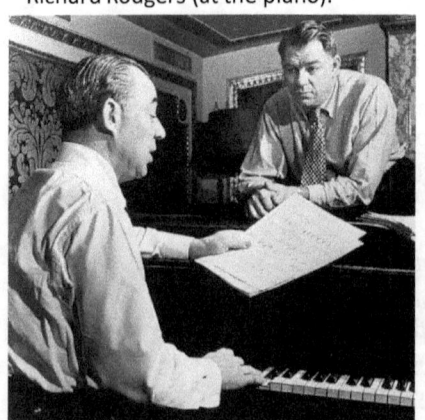

The King and I was the fifth musical by successful musical theatre team Richard Rogers (composer) and Oscar Hammerstein (lyricist). The duo were not so much concerned *if* the film would be a success, but rather if it would be a bigger success then their earlier sensation *South Pacific* (1949).

Brynner was a young newcomer when he first appeared on stage as King Mongkut in the original 1951 production. He reprised his role for the 1954 touring production, the 1977 and 1985 Broadway revivals, as well as the 1979 London production. In total Brynner played the King on stage 4,625 times.

Brynner also won an Oscar for his role in the 1956 film version of *The King and I*.

Brynner poses as the King of Siam for the CBS television series *Anna and the King*, 1972.

Lawrence and Brynner on stage for the original production of *The King and I*, 1951.

The musical continues to enthrall audiences today, having undergone a major reworking in Christopher Renshaw's 1991 Australian production. Renshaw reworked sets, costumes, and dance sequences to express a more authentic Thai experience, including all Asian performers in the Asian roles. He believed the original version was now seen as culturally insensitive and sought to create a more politically correct version. This modern version went on to win four Tony Awards for its 1996 Broadway revival, including the *Best Revival* award.

Advertisement

"RC makes you feel like new!"

says GENE TIERNEY

"RC makes you feel like new!" says Gene Tierney

Whenever I feel tired RC makes me feel like new! Yes, and I know Royal Crown Cola tastes best, too. For I compared leading colas, in an impartial taste-test, and RC won my vote! Gene Tierney.

See me in "On the Riviera" a 20th Century-Fox Picture. Color by Technicolor.

Musical Memories

Music of the early '50s was smooth and mellow, with lyrics focused on story telling and expressing heartfelt emotion. Classic pop crooners with velvety voices led us to joyous highs and the depths of despair. We had yet to discover the electrifying beats of rock 'n' roll.

Music of the early '50s fell into one of three distinct styles–country, R&B, and pop music. In 1951, there was little cross over between the styles. Radio stations focused on one genre, allowing listeners easy access to their preferred type of music.

Frankie Laine, one of the biggest stars of the decade, joined Colombia Records in April '51 becoming the highest paid singer at that time. He was best known for his ability to belt out raw, emotionally charged tunes.

Laine's career would span nearly 75 years. He covered numerous genres during that time, from big-band, to blues, jazz, rock 'n roll, and pop.

Crooner Tony Bennet rose to stardom in the early '50s with continuous jukebox favorites, making him a teen idol favorite. His career peaked in the late '50s, before fading as rock 'n roll and other genres took hold.

In future years, Bennet would make a remarkable comeback, pitching at a new MTV audience. He performed well into his 90s, most notably in collaboration with Lady Gaga (2011-2021).

Bennett was the recipient of numerous awards and honors, including a Kennedy Center Honors and a star on the Hollywood Walk of Fame.

1951 Billboard Top 30 Songs

	Artist	Song Title
1	Nat King Cole	Too Young
2	Tony Bennett	Because of You
3	Les Paul & Mary Ford	How High the Moon
4	Rosemary Clooney	Come on-a My House
5	Mario Lanza	Be My Love
6	The Weavers	On Top of Old Smoky
7	Tony Bennett	Cold, Cold Heart
8	Perry Como	If
9	Mario Lanza	The Loveliest Night of the Year
10	Patti Page	Tennessee Waltz

Nat King Cole, 1952.

Mario Lanza, circa 1950.

Perry Como, 1956.

Patti Page.

	Artist	Song Title
11	Frankie Laine	Jezebel
12	Tony Martin	I Get Ideas
13	Les Paul & Mary Ford	Mockin' Bird Hill
14	Patti Page	Mockin' Bird Hill
15	Guy Mitchell & Mitch Miller	My Heart Cries for You
16	Eddy Howard	(It's No) Sin
17	Vaughn Monroe	Sound Off
18	Dinah Shore	Sweet Violets
19	Les Paul & Mary Ford	The World Is Waiting for the Sunrise
20	Guy Mitchell & Mitch Mille	My Truly, Truly Fair

Dinah Shore, 1951.   Debbie Reynolds, 1954.

21	The Four Aces	(It's No) Sin
22	Debbie Reynolds & Carleton Carpenter	Aba Daba Honeymoon
23	Frankie Laine	Rose, Rose, I Love You
24	Del Wood	Down Yonder
25	Billy Eckstine	I Apologize
26	Patti Page	Would I Love You
27	Perry Como & The Fontane Sisters	You're Just in Love
28	Ames Brothers with The Les Brown Orchestra	Undecided
29	Phil Harris	The Thing
30	Les Baxter	Because of You

* From the *Billboard* top 30 singles of 1951.

Advertisement

Dresses from the *National Bellas Hess* mail order catalog in a mix of the "tea skirt" and "sheath" styles that were popular in the year 1951.

Advertisement

FEELS SO GOOD. Fabrics made of acetate fiber are always comfortable because acetate always feels so soft and luxurious next to the skin.

IS ACETATE LIKE ANY OTHER FIBER? No. Acetate has a unique combination of qualities. It feels like silk. Washes with ease and dries quickly like nylon. But acetate has a beautiful, graceful drape that makes clothes hang exactly right and feel so good.

WHAT ACETATE IS. Acetate is the man-made textile fiber, cellulose acetate, pioneered by Celanese Corporation of America. Better fabrics of every description are made with this modern fiber.

STAYS SO FRESH. Suits and dresses of acetate stay fresh-looking. Because acetate fibers are naturally resilient they help fabrics shed their wrinkles after wearing. That's why acetate needs less pressing.

LAUNDERS SO EASILY, DRIES SO QUICKLY. Dirt washes off acetate with ease. Just a sudsing, a rinse, and your clothes are sparkling clean—ready to smooth on a hanger to dry. If preferred, press lightly with a moderate iron.

There's a new word in Fashion...
it's <u>Acetate</u>, the beauty fiber

Five ways Acetate is important to you—

Looks lovely—feels wonderful

Drapes gracefully

Recovers from wrinkling

Launders easily—dries quickly

Dry cleans perfectly

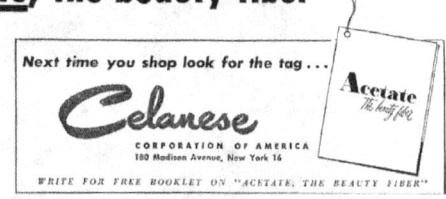

Next time you shop look for the tag...

Celanese
CORPORATION OF AMERICA
180 Madison Avenue, New York 16

Acetate
The beauty fiber

WRITE FOR FREE BOOKLET ON "ACETATE, THE BEAUTY FIBER"

Is Acetate like any other fiber? No. Acetate has a unique combination of qualities. It feels like silk. Washes with ease and dries quickly like nylon. But acetate has a beautiful, graceful drape that makes clothes hang exactly right and feel so good.

What acetate is. Acetate is the man-made textile fiber, cellulose acetate, pioneered by Celanese Corporation of America. Better fabrics of every description are made with this modern fiber.

Feels so good. Fabrics made of acetate fiber are always comfortable because acetate always feels so soft and luxurious next to the skin.

Stays so fresh. Suits and dresses of acetate stay fresh-looking. Because acetate fibers are naturally resilient they help fabrics shed their wrinkles after wearing. That's why acetate needs less pressing.

Launders so easily. Dries so quickly. Dirt washes off acetate with ease. Just a sudsing, a rinse, and your clothes are sparkling clean—ready to smooth on a hanger to dry. If preferred, press lightly with a moderate iron.

Fashion Trends of the 1950s

With the misery and bleakness of the war years behind us, the '50s were a time to show off. Consumerism was now a way of life and we were all too willing to spend money on luxuries, non-essentials, and fashion.

How we looked and how we dressed became important everyday considerations for women and men. We spent money like never before, guided by our favorite fashion icons, and helped along by a maturing advertising industry which flooded us with fashion advice through newspapers, magazines, billboards, radio and television.

We know what you want and we have it in the College Shop —

Our campus shirt — smooth-finished khaki colored cotton gabardine, 11.95
Our campus skirt — still wonderful cotton canvas with a web belt. Natural, black, dark green, rust, 14.95

The College Shop, Lord & Taylor
New York, Manhasset, Westchester, Millburn

Clothing manufacturers had perfected mass production techniques while providing military uniforms during the war years. They now shifted their focus to well made, stylish, ready-to-wear clothes.

National Bellas Hess catalog cover, 1951.

Le Petit Echo de la Mode cover, 29th April '51.

The American Weekly cover, April 1950.

Fashion was no longer a luxury reserved for the wealthy. Now the growing middle class could also afford to be fashionable. Magazines and mail-order catalogs kept us informed of the latest trends in fashion, make-up, and accessories.

Christian Dior's "New Look" from 1947.

As with before the war, all eyes looked to Paris for new directions in haute couture. In 1947 Christian Dior didn't disappoint, unveiling his glamorous, extravagant, ultra-feminine "New Look" to the world.

Gone were the boxy tailored jackets with padded shoulders and slim, short skirts. Paris had brought back femininity, with clinched waists, fuller busts and hips, and longer, wider skirts. The emphasis was on abundance. The New Look set the standard for the entire decade of the 1950s.

The "New Look" in the early '50s.

To achieve this impossible hourglass figure, corsets and girdles were sold in record numbers. Metal underwire bras made a comeback, and a new form of bra known as the "cathedral bra" or "bullet bra" became popular.

Early '50s bullet bra and girdle from Jantzen.

Despite criticisms against the extravagance of the New Look, and arguments that heavy corsets and paddings undermined the freedoms women had won during the war years, the New Look was embraced on both sides of the Atlantic. Before long, inexpensive, ready-to-wear versions of Dior's New Look had found their way into our department store catalogs.

Catalog dresses from Alden's 1954 Spring-Summer Collection.

Van Raalte
"BECAUSE YOU LOVE NICE THINGS"

News! New hues in Dark Accent* by Van Raalte

Footnotes make the headlines! Van Raalte brings you two beautiful new Forecast Colors in famous *Dark Accent* nylons. Reading from left to right: "Sea Spray," with navy heel and seam; "Sunset," with rich brown heel and seam. Reading from hem to heel: the sheerest flattery! In three fully-proportioned lengths, all with the exclusive Van Raalte Flextoe* for extra comfort and better fit. At better stores, $1.85 a pair.

Do your stockings have the Flextoe*?

Van Raalte   "Because you love nice things"
News! New hues in Dark Accent by Van Raalte

Footnotes make the headlines! Van Raalte brings you two beautiful new Forecast Colors in famous *Dark Accent* nylons. Reading from left to right: "Sea Spray," with navy heel and seam; "Sunset," with rich brown heel and seam. Reading from hem to heel: the sheerest flattery! In three fully-proportioned lengths, all with the exclusive Van Raalte Flextoe for extra comfort and better fit. At better stores, $1.85 a pair.

Do your stockings have the Flextoe?

Dior also created a slimmed down alternative look, as a sleek dress or elegant straight skirt with short jacket. This figure-hugging, groomed and tailored look, known as the sheath dress, continued to place emphasis on the hourglass figure.

Also known as the "wiggle dress", this sexier figure-hugging silhouette was preferred by movie stars such as Marilyn Monroe.

Women embraced the femininity of 1950s fashion from head to toe. Hats, scarves, belts, gloves, shoes, stockings, handbags and jewelry were all given due consideration.

Out on the street, no outfit would be complete without a full complement of matching accessories.

Advertisement

If suits of clothes were worn only once and then thrown away, like paper napkins, there might be some justification for buying the cheapest. But a suit must have a future.

It must stand up to the rigors of life and also give evidence of your good taste every time you wear it. That's why so many well-dressed men look for the *Trumpeter** label before they look for the price tag. The label is their guarantee of fine tailoring and lasting quality. The price (so often less than you expect!) is as low as that quality permits.

A Palette Tone Diagonal (shown above in a patch-pocket model) is always in quiet, good taste.

HART SCHAFFNER & MARX*

If suits of clothes were worn only once and then thrown away, like paper napkins, there might be some justification for buying the cheapest. But a suit must have a future.

It must stand up to the rigors of life and also give evidence of your good taste every time you wear it. That's why so many well-dressed men look for the *Trumpeter** label before they look for the price tag. The label is their guarantee of fine tailoring and lasting quality. The price (so often less than you expect!) is as low as that quality permits.

Not much changed in the world of men's fashion during the 1950s. Business attire shifted just a little. Suits were slimmer, and ties were narrower. Skinny belts were worn over pleated pants. Hats, though still worn, were on the way out.

Frank Sinatra.

Marlon Brando.

James Dean.

For the younger generation however, the fashion icons of the day set the trends. James Dean and Marlon Brando made the white T-shirt and blue jeans the must-have items in casual attire. Worn alone, or under an unbuttoned shirt or jacket, the look made working class style a middle-class fashion statement.

An Artificial Heart Machine October 1951

In October 1951, Professor Jacob Jongbloed from Utrecht, Holland, took to the floor at a meeting of the Congress of Surgeons, Sorbonne University in Paris, France. He presented his artificial heart machine, a mechanical heart replacement.

Long seen as the holy grail of medicine, the invention of the artificial heart machine could allow surgeons to perform life saving open heart surgery while the patient could be artificially kept alive.

Professor Jacob Jongbloed (left) explains his artificial heart machine, 1951.

The process was simple, blood would be diverted through the machine which would pump to circulate it back through the body. The patient's heart could be stopped during the period of operation.

Advances in cardiac procedures over the next few decades moved steadily. Artificial hearts and heart transplants, unimaginable back in the 1950s, are now commonplace.

Advertisement

You and your camera can give others a "visit home"

Your snapshots say it best.

When you take snapshots of Dad, or Mother, or anyone dear to the whole family, think how much these would mean to others, far and near. Extra prints in your letters are the sure tie with family and friends–especially that boy in the Service.

This year... send Photo-Greeting Cards, made from your own snapshot. Order now from your dealer.

At your dealers–dependable Kodak and Brownie cameras for snapshot opportunities ahead. For black-and-white snapshots, Kodak Verichrome Film. For full-color snapshots, Kodacolor Film.

Inaugural Pan American Games   25th Feb–9th Mar 1951

Greek athlete Aristeidis Roubanis lighting the cauldron to commence the Games, 1951.

Buenos Aires, Argentina, was the host city for the first Pan American Games in 1951.

The Games were originally proposed decades earlier by Latin American representatives of the Olympics, but the Second World War caused plans to be shelved.

The Games opened with the lighting of the cauldron with a flame from Greece, sent by the International Olympic Committee.

18 sports were offered, bringing together 2,513 participants from 14 nations. Canada did not attend but joined in later games.

Argentina won a total of 142 medals of which 63 were Gold. The USA came second with 101 medals including 46 Gold.

Chile, Cuba, Brazil and Mexico all performed well, bringing multiple medals back to their home countries.

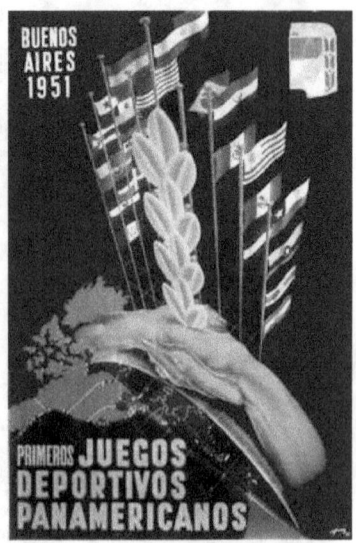

Poster for the 1951 Pan American Games.

Billed as an Olympic-style Summer competition for athletes from all the Americas, the Games are held every four years, always one year before the Olympic Games. More than 40 nations took part in the most recent Games.

Cover of *Mundo Deportivo* magazine, 15th March 1951.

Other Sporting Events from 1951

5th Apr– Ben Hogan won his first US Golf Masters Tournament. During his golfing career he would claim nine major championships and be inducted into the World Golf Hall of Fame in 1971.

5th Sep– 16-year-old Maureen Connolly Brinker won her first grand slam title at the US Open. The US teenager would prove to be one of tennis' greats, winning nine grand slams, including a golden slam in 1953. In 1954, at age 19, a horseback riding injury ended her tennis career.

10th Sep– American Florence Chadwick became the first woman to swim the English Channel in both directions.

16th Sep– American Betsy Rawls won the first of her 8 major titles at the US Women's Open, Druid Hills Golf Club, in Atlanta, Georgia.

26th Oct– Underdog Rocky Marciano defeated former champion Joe Louis by TKO in the 8th round at Madison Square Garden. He would hold the title of heavyweight boxing champion from 1952 to 1956, retiring undefeated.

11th Dec– American baseball legend Joe DiMaggio announced his retirement. He had played his final World Series game for the New York Yankees the day before.

Other News from 1951

19th-21st Jan— An unprecedented 649 avalanches in the Alps left a trail of destruction across Switzerland, Austria and Italy. Known as the "Winter of Terror", 40,000 people were buried under avalanche snow, with 265 deaths reported during the 3-month season.

3rd May— Royal Festival Hall opened as part of The Festival of Britain, a five-month national fair held in London, to promote science, technology, arts and culture.

Audience wearing 3D glasses view a stereoscopic film during the Festival of Britain.

8th May— America's first thermonuclear (hydrogen) bomb was tested at Enewetak Atoll in the new Pacific Proving Ground. This, and future tests, would pave the way for the first full scale thermonuclear bomb, tested in Nov 1952.

14th Jun— UNIVAC, (universal automated computer) became the first computer built for commercial purposes. At more than $1 million each, its relatively low cost and portability made it popular. First purchased by the United States Census Bureau, a total of 46 UNIVACs were sold by the maker Remington Rand.

20th Jul— King Abdullah I of Jordan was assassinated while attending Friday prayers in Jerusalem. The assassin, from the secret order "the Jihad", sought to prevent peace talks with Israel.
Just 96 hours earlier, a former Prime Minister of Lebanon had been assassinated for the same reason.

1st Sep– The United States, Australia and New Zealand signed a mutual defense pact known as the ANZUS Treaty. With a goal to protect the security of the Pacific, the pact has since unraveled with New Zealand and the US suspending their obligations to the Treaty.

4th Sep– The first coast to coast transmission was broadcast by CBS TV. Using state-of-the-art microwave technology, a speech delivered by President Truman in San Francisco was picked up by 87 stations in 47 cities. The speech focused on a US-Japan treaty that officially ended America's post-World War II occupation of Japan.

2nd Nov– 6,000 British troops arrived in Egypt to quell unrest in the Suez Canal. Increasing riots resulted in a state of emergency declared in Egypt the following month.

31st Dec– After distributing more than $13.3 billion in aid to rebuild Europe, the US put an end to the Marshall Plan. Also known as the European Recovery Program, the money was provided to reconstruct cities, industries and infrastructure heavily damaged during the war.

Advertisement

"My Food Budget bought the bouquet—Thanks to A&P!"

"Whoever coined that slogan, *"You can save more—more easily at A&P,"* really *has* something! There's no hunting out the best values from store to store. No comparing of quality and price each time you shop to make sure you're getting your money's worth for the prices asked. A&P's storewide values on hundreds of quality items *every day* let me shop at my convenience and enjoy savings, too. Not only that—I have confidence in everything I buy there, because A&P gives me my money back on any item I buy if I'm not *completely satisfied*. Why don't you "Test Shop" A&P? See how convenient it is to be able to buy everything you need at one store. See how much you save, too!"

Menus... All Good... Different, Too! It takes good food to make good meals—and your A&P has the widest selection of fine foods imaginable. You'll have no weekly "repeat performances" in your menus unless you prefer 'em!

See Your Savings... Check 'em, too! Prices stamped on every item at A&P show you what your spending as you shop... speed you through the checkout counter, too! Keep your cash-register slip, check and see your savings!

Give Your Food Dollars More Mileage! Remember... only about *one cent* of each dollar you spend at A&P goes for profit! Small profit is a good sign of big value... come see!

Advertisement

Standard in Travel
The new Santa Fe
Super Chief

Advanced ideas for your travel luxury... new cradled smoothness in the ride... daily between Chicago and Los Angeles

From the flanges on the wheels to the tip of the Pleasure Dome, the Super Chief is new—entirely new.

To give you the smoothest ride of your life on rails, this new Super Chief glides on cushioned springs... revises any ideas you ever had about any train.

The keynote is comfort.

You find it in the distinctive Turquoise Room in the lounge car—a delightful place to relax, enjoy a cocktail or entertain your friends at dinner—the first time such a room has been provided on any train.

You find it in the Pleasure Dome—"top of the Super, next to the stars"—that brings you an unobstructed view of wonderful southwestern scenery.

You find it in the new dining cars where Fred Harvey chefs present new and exciting menus.

Accommodations in this beautiful all-room train are designed to pamper you every mile of the way. "Push-button" radio or music in your room when you want it... beds you just can't help sleeping in... charming apartments by day.

From the engineers who glide you across this great country to the porter who answers your bell, this is the train of thoughtful service.

For your next trip between Chicago and Los Angeles say "Super Chief." Now, more than ever, it is America's train of trains. Just consult your local ticket agent.

SANTA FE SYSTEM LINES
Serving the West and Southwest

Standard in Travel   The new Santa Fe Super Chief   Advanced ideas for your travel luxury...new cradled smoothness in the ride...daily between Chigago and Los Angeles

From the flanges on the wheels to the tip of the Pleasure Dome, the Super Chief is new—entirely new. To give you the smoothest ride of your life on rails, this new Super Chief glides on cushioned springs...revises any ideas you ever had about any train. The keynote is comfort.

You find it in the distinctive Turquoise Room in the lounge car–a delightful place to relax, enjoy a cocktail or entertain your friends at dinner–the first time such a room has been provided on any train. You find it in the Pleasure Dome–"top of the Super, next to the stars"–that brings you an unobstructed view of wonderful southwestern scenery. You find it in the new dining cars where Fred Harvey chefs present new and exciting menus.

Accommodations in this beautiful all-room train are designed to pamper you every mile of the way. "Push-button" radio or music in your room when you want it...beds you just can't help sleeping in...charming apartments by day.

From the engineers who glide you across this great country to the porter who answers your bell, this is the train of thoughtful service. For you next trip between Chicago and Los Angeles say "Super Chief." Now, more than ever, it is America's train of train.

Santa Fe System Lines   Serving the West and Southwest

Famous People Born in 1951

12th Jan– Kirstie Alley, American actress.

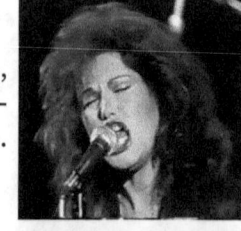

19th Jan– Martha Davis, American singer-songwriter (Motels).

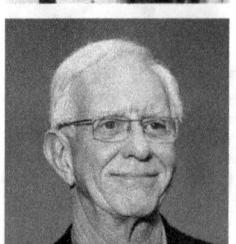

23rd Jan– Chesley Sullenberger III, American pilot (Hudson River landing).

30th Jan– Phil Collins, English drummer & singer (Genesis).

10th Feb– Robert Iger, American entertainment exec. (CEO Walt Disney).

14th Feb– Kevin Keegan, English soccer forward & manager.

15th Feb– Jane Seymour, British actress.

20th Feb– Gordon Brown, British Prime Minister (2007-2010).

4th Mar– Chris Rea, English singer-songwriter.

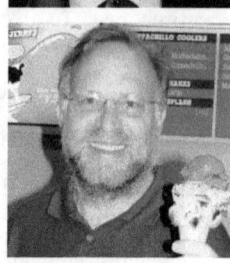

14th Mar– Jerry Greenfield, American co-founder of Ben & Jerry's ice-cream.

17th Mar– Kurt Russell, American actor.

18th Mar– Ben Cohen, American co-founder of Ben & Jerry's ice-cream.

24th Mar– Pat Bradley, American golfer (6 LPGA major titles).

24th Mar– Tommy Hilfiger, American fashion designer.

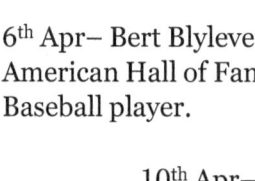
6th Apr– Bert Blyleven, American Hall of Fame Baseball player.

10th Apr– Steven Seagal, American actor.

4th May– Jackie Jackson, American singer (Jackson 5).

26th May– Sally Ride, astronaut (1st American woman to go to space).

5th June– Suze Orman, American financial advisor, writer, & television personality.

8th June– Bonnie Tyler, Welsh singer.

13th Jun– Stellan Skarsgård, Swedish actor.

3rd July– Jean-Claude Duvalier "Baby Doc", Haitian dictator-president (1971-1986).

24th Jul– Lynda Carter, American actress Miss USA (1973)

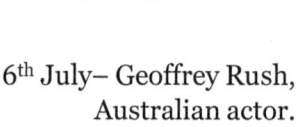
6th July– Geoffrey Rush, Australian actor.
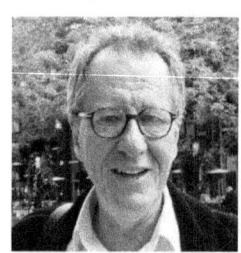

21st July– Robin Williams, American actor & comedian (d.2014).

5th Sep– Michael Keaton, American actor.

7th Sep– Chrissie Hynde, American singer-songwriter & guitarist (The Pretenders).

25th Sep– Mark Hamill, American actor (Luke Skywalker-Star Wars).

2nd Oct– Sting [Gordon Sumner], British singer-songwriter & bassist (The Police).

5th Oct– Bob Geldof, Irish singer (The Boomtown Rats) & activist (Live Aid).

7th Oct– John "Cougar" Mellencamp, American musician & actor.

14th Nov– Zhang Yimou, Chinese film director.

3rd Dec– Mike Stock, British songwriter, musician & record producer (Stock, Aitken & Waterman).

Advertisement

Help your child win success with the

World Book Encyclopedia

1st choice

of America's schools and
libraries for more than 30 years
Ask any teacher or librarian

The extra advantages your child gets at home can mean the difference between success and failure in school and, later, in life. One proved way to give your child these vital advantages is by owning the remarkable World Book Encyclopedia.

Not only is the World Book first choice of America's schools and libraries, it is praised by thousands of parents as well.

In fact, 9 out of 10 parents report it has helped their children get better school marks in an amazingly short time.

Act now to discover the wonderful difference that owning the fascinating, easy-to-use World Book can make in your child's life. Find out, too, how much your whole family will enjoy World Book and gain benefits that can't be measured in money.

More World Books are purchased annually than any other encyclopedia in America

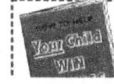 **FREE BOOKLET!** Write today for your copy of valuable FREE booklet, "How to Help Your Child Win Success." Address: World Book, Dept. 140, P. O. Box 5968, Chicago 80, Ill.

Name_____

Help your child win success with the World Book Encyclopedia 1st choice of America's schools and libraries for more than 30 years Ask any teacher or librarian

The extra advantage your child gets at home can mean the difference between success and failure in school and, later, in life. One proved way to give your child these vital advantages is by owning the remarkable World Book Encyclopedia.

Not only is the World Book first choice of America's schools and libraries, it is praised by thousands of parents as well. In fact, 9 out of 10 parents report it has helped their children get better school marks in an amazingly short time.

Act now to discover the wonderful difference that owning the fascinating easy-to-use World Book can make in your child's life. Find out, too, how much your whole family will enjoy World Book and gain benefits that can't be measured in money.

More World Books are purchased annually than any other encyclopedia in America.

1951 in Numbers

Census Statistics [1]

- Population of the world — 2.58 billion
- Population in the United States — 160.8 million
- Population in the United Kingdom — 50.6 million
- Population in Canada — 14.08 million
- Population in Australia — 8.4 million
- Average age for marriage of women — 20.4 years old
- Average age for marriage of men — 22.9 years old
- Average family income USA — $3,700 per year
- Minimum wage USA — $0.75 per hour

Costs of Goods [2]

- Average new house $9,000
- Average new car $1,500
- New Jaguar XK120 $4,039
- A gallon of gasoline $0.27
- Peanut butter $0.28
- A loaf of bread $0.18
- A gallon of milk $0.92
- Hamburger meat $0.50 per pound
- Frozen green beans $0.48 per pound
- Sliced bacon $0.55 per pound
- Eggs $0.69 per dozen
- Rice $0.17 per pound
- Cigarettes $0.20 per pack
- Movie ticket $0.47

---

[1] Figures taken from worldometers.info/world-population, US National Center for Health Statistics, Divorce and Divorce Rates US (cdc.gov/nchs/data/series/sr_21/sr21_029.pdf) and US Census Bureau, Historical Marital Status Tables (census.gov/data/tables/time-series/demo/families/marital.html).
[2] Figures from thepeoplehistory.com and mclib.info/reference/local-history-genealogy/historic-prices/1951-2/.

Advertisement

New way of handling Long Distance

Operator Toll Dialing proves a big help in these busy days of national preparedness

Long Distance lines are really humming these days. There are many more calls than a year ago. More are from the Nation's industries and Armed Forces, hurrying the country's most important job.

A big help in keeping these calls moving is Operator Toll Dialing — a remarkable new telephone development.

You give the Long Distance operator the number in the usual way. She quickly presses several keys and your call goes straight through to the telephone you want in a distant city.

It makes for faster service — especially on calls that formerly had to be relayed through other cities.

With so many more calls on the lines, it's a mighty good thing that Operator Toll Dialing was developed and is now available and in use in so many places. About one-third of Long Distance calls are now being handled in this new way.

It is just one of many ways in which the growth and improvement of telephone service are now proving of extra value to the Nation in these days of preparedness.

ANOTHER STEP FORWARD...
More and more telephone users in a growing number of metropolitan areas can now dial Toll calls direct to nearby places the same way they dial Local calls.

 BELL TELEPHONE SYSTEM

Advertisement

Nearly two million families rely on the world's most useful radio! GE Clock-Radio Wakes you to music right on the dot! How wonderful—your G-E lulls you to sleep, then wakes you the next morning to sweet music instead of a jangling alarm.

Turns itself off after you go to sleep! No more worry about falling asleep and leaving the radio on all night! It turns itself off. Even tells time in the dark.

Turns appliances on or off! Starts your coffee maker, turns on a television set and many electric appliances, automatically! Its many uses amaze you!

Here's the radio that says "Good Morning" with music and coffee. It's America's most popular clock-radio—outselling all other makes *combined!* Ideal for everyone, every day. In 4 beautiful colors—alabaster ivory, Congo brown, Persian red or porcelain white. All at the same low price! Model 516, above.

New super-powered G-E Clock-Radio, Model 535, right. Most powerful of them all—gets distant stations sharp and clear. All automatic features. Rich cordovan plastic cabinet.

You can put your confindence in—General Electric

These words first appeared in print in the year 1951.

- GUNPOINT
- Manic-depressive illness
- cargo pants
- acrylic fiber
- patented
- cable television
- WRAP-UP
- White Nationalist
- genetic engineering
- slippery slope
- hydroxychloroquine
- Murphy's Law
- teleprompter
- whiteboard
- FAST-FOOD
- SUPPORT GROUP
- trailblazing

*From merriam-webster.com/time-traveler/1951.

A heartfelt plea from the author:

I sincerely hope you enjoyed reading this book and that it brought back many fond memories from the past.

Success as an author has become increasingly difficult with the proliferation of **AI generated** copycat books by unscrupulous sellers. They are clever enough to escape copyright action and use dark web tactics to secure paid-for **fake reviews**, something I would never do.

Hence I would like to ask you—I plead with you—the reader, to leave a star rating or review on Amazon. This helps make my book discoverable for new readers, and helps me to compete fairly against the devious copycats.

If this book was a gift to you, you can leave stars or a review on your own Amazon account, or you can ask the gift-giver or a family member to do this on your behalf.

I have enjoyed researching and writing this book for you and would greatly appreciate your feedback.

Best regards,
Bernard Bradforsand-Tyler.

Please leave a book review/rating at:

https://bit.ly/1951-reviews

Or scan the QR code:

Flashback books make the perfect gift- see the full range at

https://bit.ly/FlashbackSeries

Image Attributions

Photographs and images used in this book are reproduced courtesy of the following:

Page 6 – Western Electric print advertisement from 1951. Source: eBay.com (PD image).*
Page 8 – From the *LOOK* Magazine Photograph Collection. Source: Library of Congress, Prints & Photographs Division, [Reproduction number e.g., LC-L9-60-8812, frame 8] (PD image).*
Page 9 – From the Benjamin Moore House Paint 1950s advertisement. Source: flickr.com/photos by 1950sUnlimited. Attribution 2.0 Generic (CC BY 2.0).
Page 10 – Sears Home advertisement from 1951. Source: sears-homes.com/2015/01/the-last-man-standing.html
Page 11 – Bendix advertisement, source: books.google.com/books?id=a1QEAAAAMBAJ&printsec. Pre 1978 (PD image).* – Magazine cover by Science Service Inc. Source: comicbookplus.com/?cbplus= atomic. Pre 1978, no mark (PD image).
Page 12 – From *Life* Magazine 5th Mar 1951. Source: books.google.com/books?id=0UsEAAAAMBAJ&printsec. (PD image).*
Page 13 – Victoria Embankment j/w Westminster Bridge by Leonard Bentley. Source: search.creativecommons.org/ photos/3d631476-f436-4609-86b4-875edda5c618. License CC BY-SA 2.0.
Page 14 – Children in class, creator unknown. Pre 1978, no copyright mark (PD image).
Page 15 – From *Life* Magazine 5th Mar 1951. Source: books.google.com/books?id=0UsEAAAAMBAJ&printsec. (PD image).*
Page 16 – Photo source: dp.la. Photographer unknown, US government owned image (PD image).
Page 17 – Packard, source: books.google.com/books?id=a1QEAAAAMBAJ&printsec. Pre 1978, no copyright mark (PD image).* – Studebaker, source: flickr.com/photos/andreboeni/30075178957/ by Andrew Bone. – Hudson, source: flickr.com/photos/andreboeni/26069330288/ by Andrew Bone. Attributions 4.0 International (CC BY 4.0).
Page 18 – From *Life* Magazine 9th Apr 1951. Source: books.google.com/books?id=4E4EAAAAMBAJ&printsec (PD images).*
Page 19 – From *Life* Magazine 5th Mar 1951. Source: books.google.com/books?id=0UsEAAAAMBAJ&printsec. (PD image).*
Page 20 – From *Life* Magazine 1st Oct and 3rd Dec 1951. Source: books.google.com/books?id=a1QEAAAA MBAJ&printsec and books.google.com/books?id=oVQEAAAAMBAJ&printsec (PD images).*
Page 21 – Screen stills from *The Colgate Comedy Hour*, by Colgate-Palmolive-Peet.** Source: commons. wikimedia.org/wiki/File:Dean_Martin_ Jerry_Lewis_Colgate_Comedy_Hour_early_1950s.JPG. –*The Lone Ranger* promo photo from ABC Television April 11, 1960. Pre 1978, no copyright mark (PD image).
Page 22 – *Dragnet* by NBC, screen still from Season 1, Episode 2.** – *Search for Tomorrow*, screen still by CBS.** Source: imdb.com/title/tt0043229/mediaviewer/rm1990866176. – Promo photo for *The Red Skelton Show,* by NBC.** – *Crazy People,* BBC 1951.** Source: bbc.co.uk/comedy/thegoonshow/.
Page 23 – Screen still from *I Love Lucy,* by CBS Broadcasting,** taken from the book *I Love Lucy: Celebrating 50 years of Love and Laughter,* by Elisabeth Edwards, Running Press Book Publishers, 2010. Source: Library of Congress (097.01.00). [Digital ID # lucy0097_02]. – Still Image from *I Love Lucy,* 14th Nov 1955 episode "Face to Face".** Source: wikipedia.org/ wiki/I_Love_Lucy#/media/File:I_Love_ Lucy_1955.JPG. Courtesy of Desilu and CBS Broadcasting, Inc. – Publicity photo of the *I Love Lucy* cast by CBS Broadcasting. Source: commons.wikimedia.org/wiki/Category:Lucille_Ball#/media/File:I_Love_ Lucy_Cast.JPG. Pre 1978, no copyright mark (PD image).
Page 24 & 25 – From *Life* Mag 12th Mar 1951, source: books.google.com/books?id=x0sEAAAAMBAJ& printsec & *Life* Mag 5th Feb 1951, source: books.google.com/books?id=50sEAAAAMBAJ&printsec (PD).*
Page 26 – US tank and crew, source: commons.wikimedia.org/wiki/File:HA-SC-98-06983-Crew_of_ M24_along_Naktong_ River_front-Korean_war-17_Aug_1950.JPG. Camera Operator: SGT. RILEY. – Infantrymen behind tank, source: commons.wikimedia.org/wiki/Korean_War from the U.S. National Archives and Records Administration. Images this page are US Federal Government owned (PD image).
Page 27 – F4U-4B Corsair from Air and Space Museum No. 306-FS-237-2 - U.S. Defense Imagery photo VIRIN: HD-SN-98-07598. Source: commons.wikimedia.org/wiki/Korean_War#/media/File:F4U-4B_VF-113_CV-47_1950.JPEG. – Hawker Sea Fury (Photograph was released by Commander, Naval Forces Far East on 7th June 1951) No. NH 97044. Source: commons.wikimedia.org/wiki/Korean_War#/media/File: SeaFury_launch.jpg. – Fighter bomber USAF - U.S. Defense Imagery photo VIRIN: HD-SN-98-07611. Source: commons.wikimedia.org/wiki/Korean_War#/media/File:P51_Mustang_ bombs_ NKorea_HD-SN-98-07611.jpeg. All images this page are property of the US Army, Federal Government (PD images).
Page 28 – Medical corpsmen, 1st Battalion Aid Station, 31st Infantry Regiment, 7th U.S. Infantry Division. Photo #1-4885-4/FEC-52-30954 (Sylvester). Source: commons.wikimedia.org/wiki/ File:Medical-corpsmen-korea.jpg. – US soldiers photo source: commons.wikimedia.org/wiki/File:KoreanWarFallen Soldier1.jpg. – Korean girl carrying baby brother, by Maj. R.V. Spencer, UAF (Navy).

Source: commons.wikimedia.org/wiki/File: KoreanWarRefugee WithBaby.jpg, from the National Archives & Records Administration, cataloged under National Archives Identifier (NAID) 520796. All images this page are property of the US Army, owned by the Federal Government (PD images).
Page 29 – From *Life* Magazine 14th May 1951.
Source: books.google.com/books?id=jIEEAAAAMBAJ&printsec. (PD image).*
Page 30 – Ivy Mike by The Official CTBTO, source: flickr.com/photos/ctbto/ 6476282811/. Pre 1978 (PD image). – Military personnel watch Operation Plumbbob in the Nevada Deseret, 1957. All images property of National Nuclear Security Administration. Nevada Site Office Photo Library under numbers PLU-57-100, PLU-57-031 and PLU-57-037 (PD images).
Page 31 – Nuclear explosion 1951, courtesy of National Nuclear Security Administration.
Source: en.wikipedia.org/wiki/ Nevada_Test_Site. Property of US Federal Government (PD image).
– Las Vegas tourism postcard circa 1951, creator unknown. Pre 1978, no copyright mark (PD image).
Page 32 – From *Life* Magazine 4th Jun 1951.
Source: books.google.com/books?id=b1EEAAAAMBAJ&printsec. (PD image).*
Page 33 – Rosenbergs by Roger Higgins, source: www.loc.gov/resource/cph.3c17772/ (PD image).
Page 34 – From Life Magazine 9th Apr 1951.
Source: books.google.com/books?id=4E4EAAAAMBAJ&printsec. PD image).*
Page 35 – Churchill with Randolf Churchill & Winston Spencer-Churchill, from the Library of Congress Toni Frissell Collection: LC-DIG-ppmsca-0537. Copyright released (PD image). – Churchill with Eisenhower & Montgomery, by ACME Newspictures, in the Library of Congress NY World-Telegram & Sun Collection, copyright released (PD image).
Page 36 – Danger Sign, reproduction of a farm sign in Johannesburg. 1st July 1952.
Source: commons.wikimedia.org/wiki/ Category:Apartheid_signage (PD image).
– Photo from timeslive.co.za, photographer unknown. (PD image).
Page 37 – Photo from sahistory.org.za, photographer unknown. Pre 1978, no mark (PD image).
– Photo from religiousleftlaw.com, photographer unknown. Pre 1978, no copyright mark (PD image).
Page 38 – From *Life* Magazine 5th Nov 1951.
Source: books.google.com/books?id=gFQEAAAAMBAJ&printsec. (PD image).*
Page 39 – PLA in Lhasa, author《解放军报》记者. Source: commons.wikimedia.org/wiki/File:PLA_ marching_into_Lhasa. jpg. Pre 1978, no copyright mark (PD image). – Dalai Lama, source: commons. wikimedia.org/wiki/File:Dalai_Lama_in_ 1956_in_New_Delhi.jpg by Kinsey Brothers. (PD image India).
Page 40 – From *Life* Magazine 9th Apr 1951.
Source: books.google.com/books?id= 4E4EAAAAMBAJ&printsec (PD images).*
Page 41 – *The Day the Earth Stood Still*, 1951 movie poster by 20th Century Fox.** Source: en.wikipedia.org/wiki/The_Day_ the_Earth_Stood_Still. – *The Man from Planet X*, 1951 movie poster by United Artists.** Source: en.wikipedia.org/wiki/ The_Man_from_Planet_X. – *Flight to Mars*, 1951 movie poster by Monogram.** Source: en.wikipedia.org/wiki/ Flight_to_Mars_(film) – *When Worlds Collide*, 1951 poster by Paramount.** Source: en.wikipedia.org/wiki/When_ Worlds_Collide_(1951_film).
Page 42 – Screen still from *Quo Vadis* trailer, by MGM 1951.** Source: en.wikipedia.org/wiki/Quo_ Vadis_ (1951_film)#/ media/File:Quo_Vadis_(1951)_trailer_8.jpg. – Still i from video of *The Redbook Awards,* 1953.** – Publicity Grace Kelly in 1951, on the set of *High Noon*, by United Artists (PD image).
Page 43 – *An American in Paris*, 1951 poster by MGM.** – *The African Queen*, 1951 poster by United Artist.** Source: en.wikipedia.org/wiki/The_African_Queen_(film). – *Quo Vadis*, 1951 poster MGM.**
Page 44 – From *Life* Magazine 12th Nov 1951.
Source: books.google.com/books?id=fFQEAAAAMBAJ&printsec. (PD image).*
Page 45 – Screen still of Vivien Leigh in *A Streetcar Named Desire*.** Source: en.wikipedia.org/wiki/A_ Streetcar_Named_ Desire_(1951_film). – Cinema poster from 1951.** Source: en.wikipedia.org/wiki/.
– Portrait of Marlon Brando in the theatre production of *A Streetcar Named Desire,* 27th Dec 1948. From the Library of Congress, Van Vechten Collection. Source: en.wikipedia.org/wiki/A_Streetcar_Named_ Desire#/media/File:Van_Vechten_ Marlon_Brando_image_170904.jpg (PD image).
Page 46 – From *Life* Magazine 3rd Dec 1951.
Source: books.google.com/books?id=oVQEAAAAMBAJ&printsec. (PD image).*
Page 47 – From *Life* Magazine 3rd Sep 1951.
Source: books.google.com/books?id=k04EAAAAMBAJ&printsec. (PD image).*
Pages 48 & 49 – Rogers and Hammerstein 1945 press photo, Source: commons.wikimedia.org/wiki/ File:Rodgers_and_Hammerstein_at_piano-original.jpg (PD image). – Brynner portrait by CBS, 1972.
Source: en.wikipedia.org/wiki/File:Yul_ Brynner_Anna_and_the_King_television_1972.JPG (PD image). All other images this page available by creative commons,
source: en.wikipedia.org/wiki/The_King_and_I. Pre 1978, no copyright mark (PD image).
Page 50 – From *Life* Magazine 9th Apr 1951.
Source: books.google.com/books?id=4E4EAAAAMBAJ&printsec (PD image).*
Page 51 – Frankie Laine publicity photo, 1954. Source: commons.wikimedia.org/wiki/Category:Frankie_ Laine. – Tony Bennet, source: commons.wikimedia.org/wiki/Category:Tony_Bennett (PD images).
Page 52 – Nat King Cole in 1952 by GAC-General Artists Corporation (management). Permission PD-PRE1978 (PD image). – Mario Lanzo, circa 1950. Source: en.wikipedia.org/wiki/Mario_Lanza (PD image). – Perry Como by NBC Television, 1956. Source: commons.wikimedia.org/wiki/File:Perry_Como_ 1956. Permission PD-PRE1978 (PD image). – Patti Page source: wikivisually.com/wiki/Patti_Page by

General Artists Corporation. Permission PD-PRE1978 (PD image).
Page 53 – Shore promotional photo by Paramount, 1951. Source: en.wikipedia.org/wiki/Dinah_Shore. – Reynolds photo by Bob Beerman, '54. Source: en.wikipedia.org/wiki/Debbie_Reynolds. (PD images).
Page 54 – Advert source: imgur.com/gallery/F6UwKM2. Pre 1978, no copyright mark (PD image).
Page 55 – From *Life* Magazine 12th Nov 1951.
Source: books.google.com/books?id= fFQEAAAAMBAJ&printsec (PD image).*
Page 56 – Print magazine advert for Lord and Taylor, source: eBay. Pre 1978, no mark (PD image).*
Page 57 – Fashion magazine covers from 1951. Pre 1978, no copyright mark (PD image).
Page 58 – Photo by Lars Nordin, CC BY 4.0,
Source: commons.wikimedia.org/w/index.php?curid=39208366.
Page 59 – Jantzen advert. Source: flickr.com/photos/nesster/5521936717/ Attribution 4.0 International (CC BY 4.0). – Catalog dresses from Spiegel's 1956 Spring-Summer Collection (PD image).*
Page 60 – From *Life* Mag 12th Mar 1951.
Source: books.google.com/books?id=x0sEAAAAMBAJ&printsec. (PD image).*
Page 61 – Marilyn Monroe in 1952 studio publicity portrait for film *Niagara*, by 20th Century Fox. (PD image). – Models walking photo. Source: Jessica at myvintagevogue.com. Licensed under CC BY 2.0.
Page 62 – From *Life* Magazine 5th Mar 1951.
Source: books.google.com/books?id=0UsEAAAAMBAJ&printsec. (PD image).*
Page 63 – Sinatra, source: morrisonhotelgallery.com/collections/wtvp8g/The-Sinatra-Experience-. – Brando, source: dailybreak.co/wp-content/uploads/2019/06/Marlon-Brando-Ford-Thunderbird-1955-Est.-2444.jpg. – Dean, source: en.wikipedia.org/wiki/James_Dean. All images this page Pre-1978, no copyright mark (PD image).
Page 64 – Jongbloed, 30th August 1951. Source unknown. Pre 1978, no copyright mark (PD image).
Page 65 – From *Life* Magazine 8th Oct 1951.
Source: books.google.com/books?id=jFQEAAAAMBAJ&printsec. (PD image).*
Page 66 – Roubanis lighting the torch, 25th Feb 1951. source: commons.wikimedia.org/wiki/File:Panamericanos.jpg. Pre 1978, no copyright renewal (PD image). – Poster** source: en.wikipedia.org/wiki/File:Pan_am_1951.jpg. – Magazine cover,** source: guides.library.illinois.edu/sports.
Page 67 – Hogan in a homecoming parade on Broadway, photo 21st July 1953 by Dick DeMarsico. Source: loc.gov/pictures/ resource/cph.3c15559/ rep number LC-USZ62-115559. – Connolly in 1953, from the Dutch National Archives, source: commons.wikimedia.org/wiki/Category:Maureen_Connolly#/media/File:Maureen_ Connolly_1953.jpg. – Chadwick press photo in 1951. Source: commons.wikimedia.org/wiki/Category:Florence_Chadwick#/media/File: Florence_Chadwick_ 1951.jpg. Pre 1978, no copyright renewal (PD image). – DiMaggio in a 1951 issue *Baseball Digest*. Source: commons.wikimedia.org/wiki/Category:Joe_DiMaggio#/media/File:Joe_DiMaggio_1951.png (PD image).
Page 68 – At the Telekinema, Festival of Britain 11th May 1951, from The National Archives UK record WORK25/208. Source: en.wikipedia.org/wiki/File:The_National_Archives_UK_-_WORK_25-208.jpg. Pre 1978, no copyright mark (PD image). – Greenhouse George nuclear test, 9th May 1951. From the National Nuclear Security Administration. Source: en.wikipedia.org/wiki/Operation_Greenhouse. US Federal Government photo (PD image).
Page 69 – Truman, 16th Dec 1950, from the National Archives & Records Admin (NAID) 541951. Source: en.wikipedia.org/wiki/Presidency_of_Harry_S._Truman. US Federal Gov photo (PD image). – Egypt, screen still from video *Egypt Crisis* by Brithish Pathe.** Source: youtube.com/watch?v=-zOlcHiBI9c.
Page 70 – From *Life* Magazine 9th July 1951.
Source: books.google.com/books?id=m04EAAAAMBAJ&printsec (PD image).*
Page 71 – Santa Fe System Lines print advertisement from 1951. Source: eBay.com (PD image).*
Page 72-74 – All photos are, where possible, CC BY 2.0 or PD images made available by the creator for free use including commercial use. Where commercial use photos are unavailable, photos are included here for information only under US fair use laws due to: 1- images are low resolution copies; 2- images do not devalue the ability of the copyright holders to profit from the original works in any way; 3- Images are too small to be used to make illegal copies for use in another book; 4- The images are relevant to the article created.
Page 75 – From *Life* Magazine 1st Oct 1951.
Source: books.google.com/books?id=a1QEAAAAMBAJ&printsec. (PD image).*
Page 78 & 79 – From *Life* Magazine 9th Apr 1951.
Source: books.google.com/books?id= 4E4EAAAAMBAJ&printsec & *Life* Magazine 5th Nov 1951.
Source: books.google.com/books?id=gFQEAAAAMBAJ&printsec. (PD image).*

*Advertisement (or image from an advertisement) is in the public domain because it was published in a collective work (such as a periodical issue) in the US between 1925 and 1977 and without a copyright notice specific to the advertisement.
**Posters for movies or events are either in the public domain (published in the US between 1925 and 1977 and without a copyright notice specific to the artwork) or owned by the production company, creator, or distributor of the movie or event. Posters, where not in the public domain, and screen stills from movies or TV shows, are reproduced here under USA Fair Use laws due to: 1- images are low resolution copies; 2- images do not devalue the ability of the copyright holders to profit from the original works in any way; 3- Images are too small to be used to make illegal copies for use in another book; 4- The images are relevant to the article created.

This book was written by Bernard Bradforsand-Tyler as part of *A Time Traveler's Guide* series of books.

All rights reserved. The author exerts the moral right to be identified as the author of the work.

No parts of this book may be reproduced, stored in any retrieval system, or transmitted in any form or by any means, without prior written permission from the author.

This is a work of nonfiction. No names have been changed, no events have been fabricated. The content of this book is provided as a source of information for the reader, however it is not meant as a substitute for direct expert opinion. Although the author has made every effort to ensure that the information in this book is correct at time of printing, and while this publication is designed to provide accurate information in regard to the subject matters covered, the author assumes no responsibility for errors, inaccuracies, omissions, or any other inconsistencies herein and hereby disclaims any liability to any party for any loss, damage, or disruption caused by errors or omissions.

All images contained herein are reproduced with the following permissions:
- Images included in the public domain.
- Images obtained under creative commons license.
- Images included under fair use terms.
- Images reproduced with owner's permission.

All image attributions and source credits are provided at the back of the book. All images are the property of their respective owners and are protected under international copyright laws.

First printed in 2020 in the USA (ISBN 979-8698686040).
Revised in 2021, 2nd Edition (ISBN 978-0-6450623-1-1).
& 2024, 3rd Edition (ISBN 978-1-922676-28-3).
Self-published by B. Bradforsand-Tyler.

www.ingramcontent.com/pod-product-compliance
Lightning Source LLC
Chambersburg PA
CBHW070320120526
44590CB00017B/2762